Many people helped the author in making this book possible. Special thanks are offered Gary Novickij, President, The Gym, New York City, Anita Mathieu, The Gym's manager, and Carol Elsner, the instructor there, for their cooperation; also, Marilyn Cross of the U.S. Gymnastics Federation, New York State; and photographer Michel Le Grou, Wagner International Photos. The author is also grateful to Lisa Guest, Betsy Delia, and Mia Squeri, who served as photographic models; and Francis Heilbut, Director, American Landmark Festivals; and Tim Sullivan.

BETTER GYMNASTICS

for Girls

George Sullivan

DODD, MEAD & COMPANY · NEW YORK

Frontispiece: **Jodi Yocum (left) of Reading, Pennsyl-
vania, and Kathy Howard of Oklahoma City were
among America's leading women gymnasts during
mid-1970s.**

Library of Congress Cataloging in Publication Data

Sullivan, George, 1927–
    Better gymnastics for girls.

    SUMMARY: Presents instructions for maneuvers in four
women's gymnastic events: floor exercise, balance beam,
vaulting, and uneven parallel bars. Discusses the
history of gymnastics and includes sources for further
information.
    1. Gymnastics for children—Juvenile literature.
2. Gymnastics for women—Juvenile literature.
[1. Gymnastics for women]   I. Title.
GV464.5.S84   796.4'1   77–6484
ISBN 0–396–07453–7

CONTENTS

INTRODUCTION

Most participant sports were created by men for men. They emphasize strength, stamina, and speed. Gymnastics is different. Special events have been devised exclusively for women. They stress grace, precision, and flexibility.

Women's gymnastics didn't always have the distinctive character it has today. Women used to compete in exactly the same events as men, lifting barbells and flipping about on flying rings. The Olympic Games in Helsinki in 1952 marked a turning point. Since then, women have competed in four events all their own. (A section of this book is devoted to each one of them.) They are:

FLOOR EXERCISE—Leaps, spins, and balances, plus some elements of tumbling, performed on a 40-foot by 40-foot mat to musical accompaniment. Floor exercise is often the favorite routine of gymnasts.

BALANCE BEAM—Probably the most challenging of all women's events, the beam demands not only grace and poise, but courage. Any of the dance or tumbling movements performed in floor exercise are possible on the beam, which is approximately 16 feet in length, four inches wide, and four feet above the floor.

VAULTING—Running and springing over a piece of heavily padded apparatus called a "horse," which stands about 3½ feet above the floor and somewhat

Young bodies are supple bodies. This is junior champion Katia Amsler.

resembles a sawhorse. The handspring is a typical vault, while a gymnast of Olympic-level skill might perform a half turn leading to a back somersault.

UNEVEN PARALLEL BARS—An extremely fast-moving event consisting of balances, flips, twists, and various swinging movements performed on a pair of wooden or laminated bars, one mounted about 5½ feet above the floor, the other at 7½ feet.

At what age can one begin gymnastics training? The younger the better. A girl of six or seven is likely to have the perfect body for gymnastics: tiny and supple. And by beginning the sport at an early age, a girl can take her time in developing, becoming gradually proficient in a wide range of stunts.

Girls in their early teens also have light bodies, well suited for athletics and acrobatic routines. Their weight is well balanced.

No matter one's age, there are countless values to be derived from gymnastics, some physical, others psychological. The sport, besides building strength, also improves balance, coordination, agility, and flexibility. You'll stand better; you'll walk better.

Gymnastics is also a confidence-building activity. The successful performance of a stunt, likely to require a good deal of dedication and discipline, is very much an individual accomplishment, a personal accomplishment. Joy and pride are often the direct result.

While those gymnastics events now classified as women's events are of fairly recent origin, gymnastics itself can be traced to ancient times. Most sources say that gymnastics began in Greece; in fact, the word itself is derived from the Greek. Teen-age Greek boys are said to have devoted as much time to gymnastics as they did to art and music combined. At first, gymnastics referred merely to exercises that were meant to build strength and improve skills important to other sports, but in time the exercises came to be appreciated in themselves.

Grecian girls also received gymnastics training. Their exercises included tumbling, dancing, leaping, running, rope climbing, and balance movements.

The Romans adopted the gymnasium concept after they conquered Greece. Not only did the Romans stress physical artistry, but they taught the arts and sciences within the gymnasium walls. Following the fall of the Roman Empire and throughout the Middle Ages, interest in formalized physical activity dwindled. But during the Renaissance, a renewed interest in gymnastics swept Europe.

Much of this interest was centered in Germany. Johann Guts Muhs introduced gymnastics into Prussian schools during the early 1800s, and he wrote *Gymnastics for Youth*, thought to be the first book on the subject.

Friedrich Jahn, a Prussian gymnastics director, is often hailed as the "Father of Gymnastics." He founded the turnverein movement. Turnvereins

Ornamental German stein honors Friedrich Jahn, the "Father of Gymnastics." Words "Gut Heil" mean "Good Health."

were clubs that combined gymnastics training with patriotic demonstrations. They exist to this day, both in Europe and the United States. Jahn is also credited with inventing several types of gymnastics apparatus, including the parallel bars and the vaulting horse.

Like many other American sports, gymnastics was brought to the United States by immigrants from Europe. German-Americans and Swiss-Americans established their turnvereins here; Russian-Americans and Slovak-Americans had their *sokols*, which were similar.

When, in 1865, the turnverein movement felt the need for instructors to serve its member clubs, it established the Normal College of American Gymnastics in Indianapolis. The college later became part of the University of Indiana. The Young Men's Christian Association—the YMCA—spurred the growth of gymnastics by including equipment for the sport in their gymnasiums and providing instructors. A school to train YMCA instructors was founded in Springfield, Massachusetts.

After the Amateur Athletic Union became the governing body of gymnastics in 1893, the organization helped to standardize the sport's rules and set regulations for conducting meets. More and more colleges began taking up the sport as a result.

World War II, which brought about an increased emphasis on physical training for both men and women, served to stimulate interest in gymnastics,

This costume was described as a "gymnastic suit for girl 10 to 12 years old" in an American magazine of the 1870s.

notably in colleges and high schools.

National competition in such events as the rope climb, parallel bars, and flying rings dates to the 1880s, but only males competed at that time. Not until 1931 were the first national gymnastics championships held for women. Women's Olympic competition began in 1928, but women competed only in team events, not as individuals. Individual Olympic events for women were first held in 1952.

Gymnastics took a giant step forward in 1962 when the newly formed U.S. Gymnastics Federation became the governing body of the sport. With headquarters in Tucson, Arizona, the USGF distributes information about gymnastics, conducts clinics and camps, and holds national championships.

American women gymnasts who entered international meets were all but ignored by the press and public for years. A breakthrough came in 1970, the year Cathy Rigby stunned the world of gymnastics by winning a silver medal for her performance on the balance beam in the 1970 World Championships in Yugoslavia. Never before had any American—male or female—won a medal in international competition. Cathy turned professional in 1972.

Women's gymnastics has experienced a period of mushrooming growth in recent years. The widely publicized feats of Russia's Olga Korbut in the 1972 Olympic Games and those of Romania's Nadia

Olga Korbut, an Olympic champion at sixteen.

Comaneci in the Olympics of 1976 had an enormous impact on the sport.

Olga Korbut's career as a gymnast began in 1964 when she was nine and her parents enrolled her in a school of gymnastics in Grodno, a town a few miles east of the Soviet-Polish border. Her skill and determination were such that she was soon singled out for special schooling. She began training five hours a day, six days a week, twelve months a year. She got eight or nine hours sleep a night. She was careful about her diet. Gymnastics became the most important thing in her life.

Olga was sixteen at the time of the Olympic Games in Munich in 1972. She stood 5-foot-1; she weighed 84 pounds. A pixie figure, her blonde hair in yarn-tied pigtails, she drew oohs and aahs from the spectators for her grace and daring. She won a gold medal for her floor exercise routine, another gold in the beam competition, and a silver in the bars.

When the Olympic Games shifted to Montreal in 1976, Olga was back, but she was forced to relinquish the spotlight to fourteen-year-old Nadia Comaneci (pronounced Koh-man-eech), who displayed precision and boldness of breathtaking quality. The feats that Nadia was able to accomplish with her 86-pound body had spectators gasping one minute and cheering the next.

It wasn't only the spectators who were impressed. Seven times the judges gave Nadia 10-point perfect scores for her performances. She won a gold medal in the beam competition, another for the uneven parallel bars, a third for all-around, a bronze in floor exercise (which she performed to the accompaniment of "Yes, Sir, That's My Baby"), and just missed another bronze when she placed fourth in vault.

Nadia was so good that it was often said, "You get a chill watching her." Few heroines in any sport ever so thoroughly captivated the Olympics. "Princess of the Games," she was called.

Nadia was born and brought up in Onesti, a city of 40,000 in the foothills of Romania's Carpathian Mountains. Her father was an auto mechanic, her mother an office worker. One day when she was six and playing in a courtyard during school recess, she was spotted by Bela Karolyi, a gymnastics instructor who was scouting kindergartens of Romania in search of budding gymnasts. "Nadia and her friends were running and jumping and pretending to be gymnasts," Karolyi told reporters at the 1976 Olympic Games in Montreal. (Karolyi was there as coach of Romania's women's gymnastics team.) "Then the bell rang and they ran into the building and I lost them. I went into all the classes looking

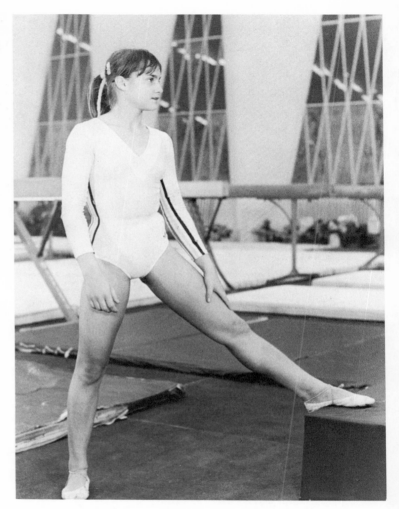

Nadia Comaneci, Romania's brilliant young Olympic gymnast.

Romanian coach Bela Karolyi and his wife Marta work with young gymnasts in their school in Onesti, Romania.

for them." Who likes gymnastics?, Karolyi asked in each class. In one classroom, two girls sprang up. One was Nadia.

So began Nadia's career. She started devoting four hours a day after school to gymnastics routines, which meant less time for her other interests, such as swimming, biking, and reading. Her strict diet limited her to fruit, milk, cheese, and other foods high in protein content, never any bread or sweets. When Nadia toured the United States with the Romanian team in the spring of 1976, an American coach noted that she ate only salads at the various luncheons and dinners given in the team's honor.

A year after her training program had begun, Nadia, then seven, placed thirteenth in her first meet. Two years later, she won the Romanian junior championship, and she continued winning in the years that followed. Her greatest triumph prior to the 1976 Olympics came in 1975 when she won the European championship. She was thirteen at the time, the youngest champion in the eighteen-year-old history of the event.

"Nadia would have made something of herself, even if it were not for gymnastics," said Bela Karolyi in 1976. "She is intelligent; she is dedicated and strong of spirit. She has a good physique, but this wasn't as important as her fire and enthusiasm.

"It is very important for a child to love gymnastics as she does. She was always a very lively child, but she never smiled very often. She was always serious and emotionally strong. I don't remember seeing her cry."

Despite her long string of championships, Nadia was continually challenged by gymnastics, and she never stopped learning exciting new routines. In New York City in the America's Cup Competition in 1976, Nadia performed a double salto, a double flip, in the floor exercise, the first woman ever to do so. She also perfected a daring back aerial somersault on the beam. Some coaches believed that she would one day perform a triple twist, considered virtually an impossible move for male gymnasts as well as female. "Nadia is capable of doing whatever she sets her mind on doing," said Frank Bare, Executive Director of the United States Gymnastics Federation.

American women have a good distance to travel before they become the competitive equals of their counterparts in Russia, Romania, East Germany, Hungary, and some other Eastern European coun-

tries. At Montreal in 1976, the United States women's gymnastics team finished sixth. Russia was first, Romania second. American women finished eleventh in both floor exercises and the vault, and eighteenth in the bars and beam.

Why are Americans so overshadowed? One reason is financial. Russian gymnasts, for example, are subsidized as "National Masters of Sports," their lessons and travel expenses paid for by the government. "The Russian girls have got it made," said one disgruntled member of the 1976 American Olympic team. "Not only do they get financial support, but there's one coach for every two gymnasts. They even have choreographers from the Russian ballet help them in developing their routines."

An American gymnastics competitor not only has to pay tuition and instruction fees at a private club, but also travel, lodging, and registration fees for national meets. "We seem to penalize rather than reward our best athletes," says one coach.

The situation has scarcely affected the growth of interest in the sport. The number of private gymnastics clubs, put at 50 in 1970, had jumped to 500 by 1976. At the junior national championships in 1976, there were 138 entries in the 13 to 14 age classification, more than twice as many as were entered six years before.

As for the total number of gymnasts, it increased from 45,000 in 1970 to approximately 500,000 in 1976. Somewhere among them perhaps there is another Olga Korbut or Nadia Comaneci.

WARMING UP

It's essential to warm up before attempting any gymnastics exercise. Warming up prepares your body for the work it is to do. Should you attempt to work out without a proper warm-up, you increase the risk of injury.

Most of your warm-up period should be devoted toward extending your range of movement, that is, toward increasing the flexibility of your muscles. A few of the many exercises that are meant to accomplish this are pictured on these pages.

They are all stretching exercises. Each should be performed smoothly and easily. Forcing yourself can cause a painful muscle strain. Suppose that you are seated on the floor, your legs stretched out in front of you, and you plan to touch your head to one knee without bending the legs. Slowly bend your head downward toward the knee. When you've moved your head down as far as you can, hold the position for a few seconds, then attempt to go a bit farther. Take your time. Never use quick, jerky movements when attempting this or any other stretching exercise.

Many stretching exercises begin from a sitting position, the feet together. Bend forward as far as you can. Reach forward with both arms. Keep your legs straight.

Tricks common to floor exercise, the beam, and the vault often involve stretching both legs in opposite directions at right angles to the body—doing a split. To prepare for such tricks, stand with one foot in front of the other and slowly spread your legs so as .to lower yourself into a split position. Use your

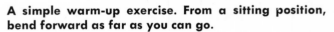

A simple warm-up exercise. From a sitting position, bend forward as far as you can go.

In the regular split, the legs are positioned in opposite directions at right angles to the body.

hands to cushion your landing, if you want. This exercise stretches the hamstring muscles at the back of the thigh and the hip flexors at the front of the thigh.

The straddle split is another good warm-up exercise. In this, the legs are stretched out to the sides. Once you're in straddle split position, bend your

This is the straddle split. Once you've taken the split position, try bending your upper body, first to one side, then to the other.

The back bend helps develop the deep arch necessary to performing such tricks as the limber and walkover.

upper body toward one side, then toward the other.

The back bend is still another warm-up exercise that many gymnasts do. First, lay on your back. Then bend your knees, bringing your feet close to your seat. Place your hands on the floor close to your shoulders. Push upward from your hands and feet so that your back forms an upside-down arch. Last, straighten your legs.

FLOOR EXERCISE

The term "floor exercise" refers to any sequence of tumbles, leaps, balances, and dance movements which, when blended together, make for a graceful and dynamic gymnastics performance.

No apparatus is involved, only a mat and open space. The area in which the routine is performed measures 12 meters by 12 meters, or about 40 feet on each side.

A floor exercise routine varies in length from 1 to 1½ minutes. A piano, or any one musical instrument, furnishes the music. The music can be recorded, and usually is.

In judging floor exercise competition, judges look for good posture, proper technique, continuity, and variety. Each performer is rated in tenths. Typical scores are 8.7, 8.9, 9.4, and 9.6. A score of 10.0 is perfect. (This scoring system is also used in judging performances on the vault, beam, and bars.)

Four judges score an event, but the ratings of only two of them are counted. The highest and low-

Katia Amsler in a floor exercise exhibition at Castle Clinton, New York City.

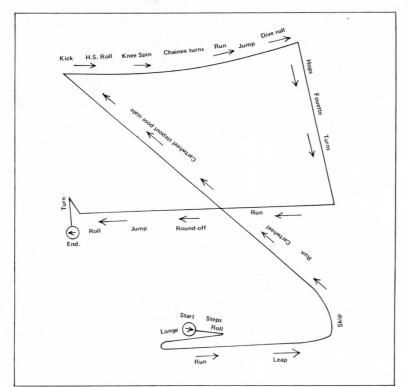

Kick H.S. Roll Knee Spin Chainee turns Run Jump Dive roll

Hops

Fouette

Turns

Cartwheel stepout pose scale

Turn

Roll Jump Round-off Run

End.

Cartwheel

Run

Skip

Start Steps

Lunge Roll

Run Leap

This pattern of floor exercises is suggested for beginners.

est scores are ignored. The scores of the other two judges are averaged to produce the recorded score. The difference between the two scores that are averaged cannot exceed certain limits. When it does, the score of a fifth judge, the head judge, is used in figuring the final score.

In team competition, the six members of each team perform compulsory and optional exercises on each of the four pieces of equipment. The five highest scores are added together to get the team total.

Many tumbling skills are involved in floor exercise routines. Tumbling is also important to routines on the balance beam and in vaulting. The pages that follow describe basic tumbling skills.

Forward Roll, Tuck Position

The forward roll is one of the basic tumbling exercises. Try it from a tuck position first, your knees bent, your upper body erect, your arms fully extended.

Put your hands to the mat, keeping them about shoulder width apart. Lower your head, putting your chin almost to your chest. This rounds your back, making the roll possible.

Push from your feet, lifting your hips and shifting your weight to your hands. You power the roll by pushing with your hands. As you go over, the back of your head touches the mat first, and then you roll onto your shoulders and back. End in a tuck position.

Begin with your knees bent; your arms fully extended. As you go over, the back of your neck touches first, then you roll on your shoulders and back. End as you began, in a tuck position.

Backward Roll, Tuck Position

It may seem odd, but in order to roll backward, you have to lean forward, at least at the beginning of the exercise.

Start from the tuck position. Rock forward, reaching with your hands, and then backward into the roll. Tuck your chin to your chest so as to round your back.

As you begin to roll, put your hands to the mat. Keep your elbows in. Push from the hands—push firmly—so as to lift your head and shoulders from the mat. Bring your feet under your body and return to a tuck position.

Lean forward slightly, then rock backward into the roll. Place your hands down forward of your shoulders. Pushing with your hands, roll over onto your feet.

Forward Roll, Straddle Position

Stand erect when beginning this roll, your legs well apart. Bend from the waist and put your hands flat to the floor, getting them as close to your body as you can.

Put your chin to your chest as you begin the roll. In the initial stages, your hands support the body's weight; then the shoulders take the weight. Keep the legs straddled.

As you come out of the roll, push from your hands to boost yourself up into the straddle position again.

In the forward straddle roll, the body's weight is first supported by the hands, then by the shoulders. Pushing from the hands enables you to thrust yourself into a straddle position again.

Reach through your legs and place your hands on the floor. As your weight goes back and the roll begins, shift your hands to a position forward of the shoulders. Push yourself into a straddle position again.

Back Roll, Straddle Position

Begin with your legs wide apart. Bending from the waist, reach through your legs to place your hands on the floor, shifting your weight back as you do. Your fingers should point forward.

Support your weight with your hands, lower your body to the mat.

As the roll begins, quickly shift your hands, bringing them to a position just forward of your shoulders. Then push to a straddle position again.

Once you've kicked up into the handstand, straighten your arms and legs. To perform the roll . . .

Handstand Roll

The art of balancing on your hands with your feet in the air is not difficult to master once you get used to the feeling of being in an upside-down position.

An exercise called the mule kick will help you to get an idea of what the handstand is going to feel like. From a standing position, reach down and put your hands to the floor, and at the same time kick up with one leg. As that leg goes down, kick up with the other leg. Keep kicking higher and higher until you begin approaching a vertical position.

In performing a handstand roll, begin by kicking up into a handstand position. First, thrust your hands above your head, then stride forward and, bending your front knee, reach down for the mat. As your hands touch down, kick your free leg upward. The other leg follows.

Extend the legs straight up. Get your arms

. . . lower your head to the mat, tuck your chin to your chest, and roll onto your shoulders and back.

straight, too.

To come out of the handstand into the roll, lower yourself to the mat until your head just touches. Keep your legs straight over your head. Tuck your chin to your chest, rounding your shoulders. Roll over onto your back, bending in the knees as you do.

Get your feet close to your seat. Push to a standing position.

Headstand Roll

When you do a headstand, your head and hands form a tripod that supports your feet in the air.

Begin from a tuck position. Put your hands to the mat in front of your body, keeping them about shoulder width apart.

Tilt forward so as to bring the top of your head in contact with the mat. Raise your legs. Now your

It's vital to form a solid base with the hands and head before attempting to raise the legs. In performing the headstand roll, first bring your chin to your chest, rounding your back. Snap to a salute at the end.

head starts bearing some of the body's weight. Extend your legs upward slowly.

If you're unsteady, start over. It's important that you be well balanced in the beginning. Otherwise, you won't be successful.

Come out of the headstand with a forward roll. Put your chin to your chest, then roll onto your shoulders, bending your knees as you do. Spring forward to a standing position.

Cartwheel

The cartwheel is a handspring in which the body turns over sideways, the arms and legs spread like the spokes of a wheel.

Begin from a standing position. Raise your arms and spread your legs. Point your left foot (if you're cartwheeling to the left) in the direction that you're going to spring. Your weight should be over the other foot.

Reach to the left with the left hand, shifting your weight to the left leg. Kick up with the right leg as you touch down with the left hand. Then the right hands touches down. Split your legs wide apart, but keep them perfectly straight. Keep your arms straight, too.

Land on the right foot, then the left. Return to a standing position.

In performing a cartwheel, you move to the side, not forward. Keep your hands and legs straight as you wheel over. The wider you split your legs, the better.

One problem that beginners have with the cartwheel is failing to get the hips high enough. A spotter can help you overcome this by standing in back of you, grasping you at the waist, and raising your hips to the proper height. This serves to impart the proper "feel" of the hip position and should make it easier for you to do the exercise correctly.

Dive Roll

Because it prepares you for advanced stunts and for vaulting, too, the dive roll is an important trick.

The dive roll can be performed either from a standing-still position or following a run-and-jump takeoff. The last named method is the one described and pictured here.

Like any stunt with a running approach, a good dive roll depends on the proper execution of a hurdle. The hurdle is the final phase of the approach, the means by which you get your body into the air and drive it forward.

The hurdle is easy to do. Following a running approach of several steps, skip with one foot, then quickly bring the other foot forward, landing on the mat with both feet simultaneously.

Bend in the knees as you land. Spring forward and upward.

Be sure to run aggressively in your approach.

Hurdle phase of the dive roll follows a running approach and involves a quick skipping step, then a jump that thrusts the body forward.

Keep in mind that what you want to do is drive your body forward. This may help you to get a more efficient hurdle.

From the hurdle, dive toward the mat, keeping your hands well apart as you land. Imagine you're diving over a barrel that's laying on its side.

Your arms act to cushion the impact of your landing, then ease your head to the mat. Tuck your chin to your chest as you roll; bend in the knees.

Your momentum will roll you to your feet. Snap to a salute as you come erect.

As you land, your arms cushion the impact, then work to lower your head to the mat. Momentum generated by the approach and hurdle powers the roll.

In executing a limber, first kick to a handstand. Then, allow the legs to drop together toward the mat. . . .

Forward Limber

The limber is a trick that is similar to a handstand. But instead of rolling out, you allow your legs to drop into an arched position before the feet touch down. Learning the limber is important to performing some advanced skills, such as the walkover.

As the feet touch, the hands push off. End in an upright position.

Take a step and kick into a handstand. Bring your legs together directly over your head; hold the position for a split second.

Then let both legs drop forward together, form-ing an arch. Just as your feet touch down, push from the mat with your hands.

Last, swing to an erect position, your arms up-stretched.

The roundoff begins with a hurdle which leads to a cartwheel, then a handstand. A quarter turn of your body follows, so that you end up facing the direction opposite from which you started.

Roundoff

The roundoff is a trick that is somewhat similar to the cartwheel. However, it also involves a handstand and a quarter turn of the body. It is used to develop speed and change the body's direction during the performance of a routine.

The roundoff begins with a running approach and a hurdle.

As you spring out of the hurdle, reach for the

mat with one hand and then the other—as in the cartwheel. The legs kick up.

When the legs are directly overhead, hold them in a handstand position for an instant.

Then snap the legs downward toward the mat with a quarter turn. Push off with your hands.

You will land in a straight up and down position facing in the direction opposite to the one in which you started.

Forward Walkover

The forward walkover is similar to and involves many of the skills of the limber.

Begin from a standing position. Stride forward and kick up from the rear leg to a handstand. But instead of keeping the legs together, one foot should be positioned well ahead of the other. In fact, the wider the split, the better.

Split the legs well apart as you perform the forward walkover. As the front foot touches down . . .

. . . push off with the hands. The head and arms come up, and then the other foot touches down.

As the forward foot touches down, push off with the hands. Then the other foot touches down. The hands finish up over the head.

The forward walkover and variations of it are used frequently in floor exercise routines. Sometimes the walkover is performed with a leg switch, that is, the position of the legs is reversed as the stunt is being performed. The handstand position has to be held a bit longer in order to have time to perform the switch. The starting and finishing positions are the same.

Another variation is the forward dive walkover. It begins with a hurdle and a vigorous push-off which springs you into the air. You land on your hands; your legs are in a stride position. The finish is the same as in the forward walkover.

The back walkover also features the legs in a stride position. You begin with one foot in front of the other, your arms over your head, and your weight concentrated over the rear leg. The head bends back to start the stunt. As the forward leg is raised, the hands reach for the mat. You push off with the other foot to get the hips up.

Once you're skilled in performing a forward walkover, a forward handspring should not be difficult for you. The handspring is a stunt in which the body is flipped completely forward from an upright position; you land first on your hands then on your feet.

Begin with a running start and execute a hurdle. As you land, bend one knee and get both hands to the mat. Keep your arms straight.

As your legs pass through a vertical position, push off with your hands. The push has to be a vigorous one. This, plus the momentum generated by the hurdle, is what flips you over. Land on both feet and come to a standing position. Throughout, keep your legs together.

Some coaches teach the front handspring by having students first perform the stunt over a rolled-up mat. After a running start and a hurdle, the hands are placed on the floor just in front of the mat, and the student springs over it, landing on her feet. As in the conventional handspring, it's important to keep the arms straight and push off forcefully with the hands.

BALANCE BEAM

"For floor exercise, you need to have a graceful, exciting routine for the judges," says Ann Carr, who won two bronze medals in representing the United States at the 1974 World Gymnastics Championships held in Russia. "On the uneven bars and in vaulting, you have to be supercharged for a display of energy and power. On the balance beam, it's all coordination and concentration."

When you mount the beam and begin your routine, your working area measures 10 centimeters (about 4 inches) in width and 5 meters (about 16 feet, 4 inches) in length. The beam is 16 centimeters (6½ inches) thick, and is mounted on supports which place it 120 centimeters (about 4 feet) above the floor.

Almost any stunt that can be done as a floor exercise can be performed on the beam. But, naturally, movement on the beam is slower and more controlled.

Be sure you master your tricks on the floor before you try them on the beam. For practice purposes, many schools and gyms offer a special low beam, which is only about a foot off the floor. Or most beams of standard height can be lowered. Use a low-level beam before trying the high beam.

Work with an instructor when you mount the beam for the first time. And even after you become skilled and experienced, have an instructor at your

Practice your stunts on a low-level beam first.

side any time you attempt a new or difficult stunt.

Get used to the fact that you are going to fall off the beam occasionally. Even veteran performers fall. Be sure there are mats covering the floor on both sides of the beam. There should also be mats at the beam ends when you are practicing dismounts.

Before you try any exercises on the beam, become fully acquainted with it. Walk back and forth on it; stand on one foot, then the other. Practice mounting and dismounting.

Don't look directly downward when you're atop the beam. Instead, keep your chin up; look straight ahead.

In beam competition, each performer presents a routine consisting of balances, turns, dance steps, jumps and leaps, plus some tumbling tricks, all sandwiched between an appropriate mount and dismount. The time limit for a beam routine varies from 1 minute and 20 seconds to 1 minute and 45 seconds. Besides technical excellence, judges expect the routine to be presented with grace and zest.

Front Support Mount

Every routine on the balance beam begins with one of several mounts. A dismount ends the routine. There are mounts and dismounts for every level of skill and experience.

One of the easiest to learn is the front support mount. Stand facing the beam, your arms at your

In executing a front support mount, spring to this position, your hands supporting your weight.

For a one-knee mount, one knee rests on the beam; the hands support the body's weight.

side. Place your hands on the beam, keeping them about shoulder width apart.

Sink in your knees and spring to a position where your arms are supporting your weight and your thighs are resting on the beam. Hold your chin up and arch your body, pointing your toes.

One-Knee Mount

The one-knee mount begins just as the previous mount did. Stand facing the beam, your hands on the beam about shoulder width apart.

Spring to an arm support position, placing one knee on the beam. The other leg should be stretched out in back of you. Keep your weight concentrated on your hands.

Squat Mount

This mount, also called a tuck vault mount, requires a short approach, usually three steps. The legs are pulled up to the beam between the arms. Sometimes this mount is performed with the aid of a special vaulting board known as a "reuther board" or beat board.

Position yourself several feet from the beam. Stand erect, your hands at your sides. Plan to take a three-step approach, hurdle, and spring to the beam, both feet landing simultaneously.

Approach the beam briskly. As you near it, reach

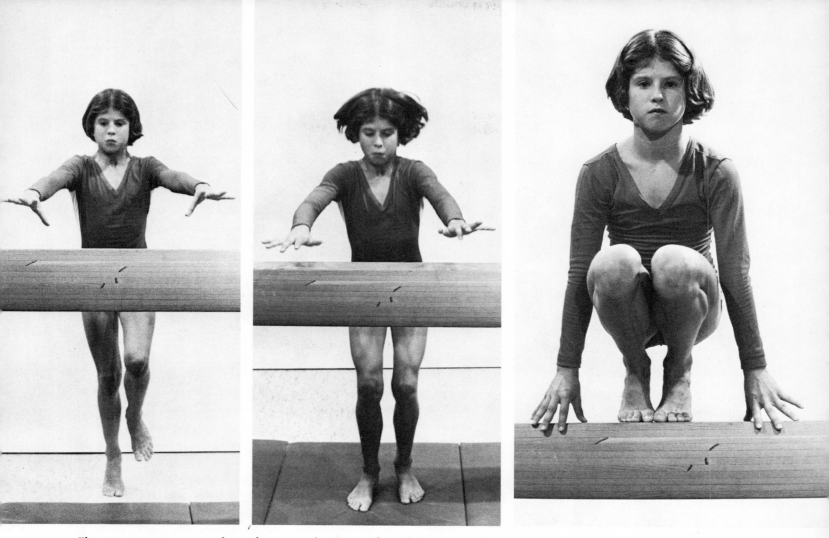

The squat mount, or tuck vault mount, begins with a short approach. Both feet are pulled up and placed on the beam between the hands.

39

For a step-up mount, after building speed with your approach, take off on your left foot; swing the right leg up, touching down with the right foot. Use your right hand, too.

out for it with both hands. Use the momentum generated by your approach and hurdle to drive your body upward. You have to obtain sufficient height to enable you to swing your feet onto the beam.

Keep your feet together as you place them on the beam. Then remove your hands and strike a posed position.

Step-up Mount

The step-up mount requires a quick burst of energy to power your body to beam level. You can do it with or without the use of the reuther board.

Approach the beam obliquely, that is, at an angle of about 45 degrees. If you're going to use the reuther board, place it at the same angle that you plan to use in your approach.

Your approach should be several steps in length, sufficient to build up good speed. Plan to take off from the left foot, lifting the right leg, then swinging the right foot onto the beam. Use your right hand, too, placing it on the beam to assist your takeoff.

Movements on the Beam

Every routine on the beam includes an assortment of steps, jumps, and turns. Each has to be performed with grace and style.

Even the simplest walking step must be executed so that it adds interest and attractiveness to the routine. The body should be kept straight, the toes pointed. The arms should swing freely and gracefully or be held in any one of several ballet positions.

The dip step is sometimes used. In this, you bend one knee, permitting the free foot to swing slightly below the beam's top surface.

You can run on the beam, too. Use short steps at first.

Turns not only enable you to change direction on the beam, but they add variety to your performance. Practice turns on the floor, using a chalked or taped line to represent the beam.

The pivot turn is the easiest turn of all. Stand on the beam with the heel of one foot just in front of the toe of the other. Rise up on the balls of your feet

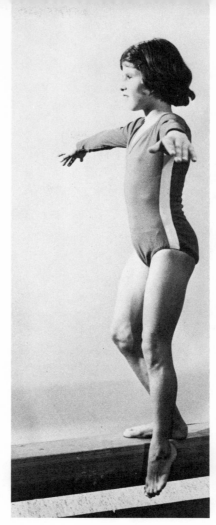

All walking steps (right) should be performed with grace and style. A dip step (left).

41

The squat turn. Get your arms out in front of your body. Pivot around on the balls of your feet.

and pivot to the left until your toes are facing in the opposite direction. Sometimes this is called a two-footed pivot turn or a tiptoe turn.

The same type of turn can also be executed from a squat position. You simply squat down with the feet positioned as described above, the heel of one foot in front of the toes of the other. Rise to the balls of your feet and pivot around.

A wide variety of leaps and jumps can be executed on the beam. The stride leap, a striking

The stride leap. You spring from one foot, perform a split, then land on the other foot.

maneuver, is among the first most gymnasts attempt. But it's not easy.

Position yourself at one end of the beam with your arms outstretched. Take a crisp stride forward. As the front foot touches down, swing the other leg forward and spring into the air.

As you reach the top of the leap, your legs should be spread apart in a stride position. (Sometimes this stunt is called a stride leap.) Keep your arms outstretched as you land.

In doing a forward roll from a standing position, bend one knee and reach for the beam sides. . . .

Forward Roll

The forward and backward roll, the handstand, headstand, handspring, cartwheel, and walkover— all of these and other tumbling exercises can be performed on the beam. Naturally, it takes confidence and courage to do advanced tricks.

Beginners on the beam are frequently taught the forward roll. Begin from a standing position. Bending one knee, reach forward to grasp the beam sides. Keep your back straight, the other leg upstretched.

44

Tuck your head; roll over on your shoulders and back, then come erect.

Place the back of your head on the beam. Tuck your chin to your chest. Push off with your foot, rolling over onto your shoulders and back. Continue the roll so that you finish in a lying down position or in a one-leg squat.

You can also begin the forward roll from a kneel-ing position or from a squat. The backward roll is performed in much the same fashion as the forward roll, your hands grasping the beam sides to assist you.

45

Roundoff Dismount

There are countless ways of dismounting from the beam. Simple jump dismounts are the first taught.

In these, you stand at one end of the beam and leap up and out, striking any one of a number of positions while in the air. You can execute a stag leap, extending the back leg and bending the for-

ward knee. In the tuck leap, both knees are brought to the chest, and the arms are stretched back. The stride leap and the straddle leap are self-descriptive.

Always land on the balls of your feet, sinking in the knees to absorb the impact. Then assume a standing position, your feet together, your arms upstretched.

The roundoff dismount is a stunt for gymnasts with some experience. It involves both a cartwheel

and a handstand and quarter turn of the body.

Step with your right foot toward the beam end. Your arms are upstretched. Bend the right knee, and reach for the upper surface of the beam with both hands.

Push off into a cartwheel. Bring your legs together so that your body assumes a handstand position.

Then push off from your hands. Execute a quar-

Begin by taking a step toward the beam end. After your foot is planted, reach for the beam with both hands, then spring from a cartwheel into a handstand. Push off with your hands, executing a quarter turn in the air, so that you land facing the beam.

ter turn as your legs snap down. Finish so that you are facing the end of the beam.

VAULTING

Vaulting is exciting and challenging. Each vault consists of a run, a hurdle, and a jump from the reuther board over a two-legged piece of gymnastic equipment with a padded body known as a "horse."

In women's vaulting, the horse is 40 centimeters (about 16 inches) in width, and 160 centimeters (5 feet, 3 inches) in length. The distance from the top of the horse to the mat is 110 centimeters (3 feet, 7 inches).

Some horses are equipped with pommels or grips. But a horse of this type is meant only for men's gymnastics. The grips are removed for women's vaulting.

Special mats, called "crash pads," are used to cushion your landing when vaulting. These are mats of more than the usual thickness and so constructed that they can absorb a great amount of impact. Standard mats of double or triple thickness are sometimes used when crash pads are not available.

The first vaults that you'll be doing won't require great running speed in the approach, but you'll still have to move briskly and smoothly. Look straight ahead as you run. Lean forward. Lift your knees on each stride. Swing your arms to increase your momentum. All of your strides should be about the same size.

Know in advance exactly where you plan to put your foot down in triggering the hurdle. The same

Vaulting involves use of a reuther board, sometimes called a beat board.

foot should serve as the take-off foot in each vault. Most right-handed gymnasts feel more comfortable using the left foot as the take-off foot.

To get the feeling of using the vaulting board, try this exercise: Take several running steps, hurdle, hit the board with both feet and place both hands on the top of the horse, tilting your body forward and driving your hips up. Then simply fall back onto your feet. Try this a number of times, going a bit higher on each try.

In standard vaults, the hands serve as a pivot from which the body springs over the horse. The hands also act to push the body upward.

In first attempts at vaulting, work with a spotter.

Keep your arms and wrists straight as your hands touch down. Your fingers should point straight ahead.

In your first attempts at vaulting, you should work with a spotter, an instructor who assists you in clearing the horse and landing. It will help you to build confidence.

Unlike the other events in women's gymnastics, vaulting does not involve the development of a routine. In competition, different vaults, some compulsory, others optional, are performed by each contestant, and a point value is assigned to each. Contestants get two chances to perform each vault, and the best score is the one recorded. The highest possible score for a vault is ten, as it is in other events.

Squat Vault

In the squat vault, as the name implies, the body is in a tucked position as you spring over the horse. The feet swing through without coming in contact with the horse.

Get a good run and hurdle. Land on the reuther board with both feet; sink in the knees and spring forward, driving the hips high. As your hands make contact with the horse, begin drawing your knees to your chest. Keep your arms straight.

Springing from the hands, swing the legs through. Then push off from your hands.

In the squat vault, your body is tucked as you spring over the horse. Stand erect as you land, your hands over your head.

Position your hands like this as you vault over.

Your body begins to straighten as you prepare to land. Tilt back slightly so you'll be better able to finish in a balanced position.

While the squat vault is not used in competitive gymnastics, it includes many of the basic principles of vaulting. By mastering it, you'll be preparing yourself for many of the more advanced vaults.

Straddle Vault

The straddle vault is similar to the squat vault. But instead of keeping your knees together and swinging your legs inside your arms, you spread your legs as you clear the horse.

After your run-up and hurdle, land on the reuther board with both feet; sink in the knees; spring forward and up. Again, you must drive the hips high.

As your hands reach out and make contact with the horse, spread your legs apart. Your legs should be well apart as they clear the horse.

As you push off from the horse, snap your legs together. Bend your knees slightly as you land. Keep your feet together.

In the straddle vault, your legs are spread as you clear the horse. Land with your feet together, your arms outstretched.

Don't try the handspring vault unless you're skilled and experienced. You need an explosive takeoff.

Handspring Vault

The handspring vault, in which the body flips over the horse from the hands, is an advanced vault.

It requires a fast approach and an explosive takeoff.

As you spring from the reuther board, reach for the horse with both hands. Let your momentum drive your legs upward.

Once in handstand position, arch your back and flip over onto your feet. Come erect, hands overhead.

Keep your legs straight until your feet are directly overhead. Then arch your back slightly and begin your descent. Land with your feet together, your arms upstretched.

UNEVEN PARALLEL BARS

When girls and women first tried gymnastics, they used the parallel bars that were common to men's competition, bars that were mounted on the same plane. But it wasn't long before it was found that parallel bars placed at different levels were better suited for women. Bars of this type put a greater emphasis on swinging and circling, in which women excel, and diminished the need for strength, for muscular power.

Uneven parallel bars began to be used in competition in the 1930s. They gained official acceptance when they were used in the Olympic Games in 1952.

The high bar of the two is mounted 2.30 meters (about 7 feet, 6½ inches) above the floor. The low bar is 1.50 meters (about 4 feet, 11 inches) above the floor.

While the height of the bars may not be changed, the distance between the bars (as measured from one set of supports to the other) can be adjusted so as to suit the gymnast's height and other physical characteristics. The rules permit the distance between bars to vary from 54 centimeters (about 21 inches) to 78 centimeters (about 30 inches).

The amount of flex a bar has is also important. A bar with a good amount of "give" to it can serve to increase your speed and momentum as you perform a routine. And such a bar produces less muscle strain. Generally speaking, the more use a bar has

Gymnastics chalk will help you to protect your hands. Also apply chalk to the bars.

54

had, the more flex it is likely to boast.

Mats should be laid out beneath the bars, and they should extend beyond the bars themselves to provide for safe landings when dismounting. Some instructors advise mats of double thickness in dismount areas. Before using a bar, be sure to check the adjustments and see that they are all tight.

To protect your hands, coat them with gymnastics chalk before using the bars. It's a good idea to apply chalk to the bars, too. Never wear rings when using the bars.

A complete routine on the bars is likely to consist of 12 to 18 different movements, all performed in less than a minute. It begins with a mount, then proceeds to stunts on the low bar, stunts on the high bar, between the bars, and, last, a dismount. The stunts include swinging, circling, and various twisting movements. Some of these are described on the pages that follow.

Front Support Mount

Using your hands and arms to raise your body onto the low bar is perhaps the easiest method of mounting the bars.

Stand erect facing the low bar. Grasp the bar in what is called a "regular grip." Your palms face away from your body as you grip. (The reverse grip is just the opposite; your palms face your body as you grip.)

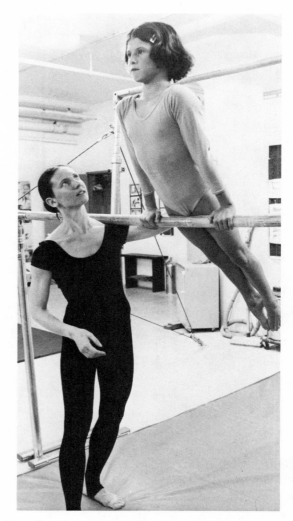

Your hands and upper thighs support your weight.

For a hip circle mount, stride toward the bar and take a firm grip.

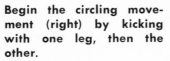

Begin the circling movement (right) by kicking with one leg, then the other.

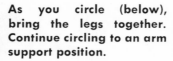

As you circle (below), bring the legs together. Continue circling to an arm support position.

Bend your knees, then spring up, pushing from your hands and straightening your arms.

In the support position, your body's weight should be supported by your hands and your upper thighs. Keep your chin up. Your back should be slightly arched, your toes pointed.

Hip Circle Mount

This mount begins with a one-step approach to the bar and involves a quick circling movement that brings you to a front support position.

As you stride, reach for the bar. Take hold and begin pulling, kicking one leg over the bar and then the other. Bring the feet together. Circle the bar and finish in an arm support position.

If the stunt seems difficult, work with a spotter. The spotter will help you in lifting your hips and assist you in circling the bar.

Pull Over High Bar

This stunt begins from a sitting position on the low bar; your hands are gripping the high bar.

Swing slightly forward, planting the left foot on

Right: In moving to the high bar from the low bar, kick off from the low bar, swing forward, and whip one leg and then the other over the high bar. Last, take an arm support position.

the low bar. As you continue to swing, drive off the left foot, pulling vigorously with your hands and arms, and kick the right leg over the top bar. Curl your hips around the bar, circle it, and come to a front support position.

Cast

The cast is a skill that is basic to almost all bar swinging movements. It involves thrusting—"casting"—your body away from a hand support position.

To execute a cast, begin from a front support position on the low bar. Swing your legs down and under the bar, then back, extending them to the rear. Your arms should be straight.

As your legs swing up, push your body away from the bar. From your hands to your toes, your body should be parallel to the floor.

Kip

The kip is another skill that is basic to stunts on the parallel bars.

You execute a kip when swinging from your hands. At the end of a swing, thrust your legs forward and upward, bending sharply at the hips. Then swing back, straightening your legs. Let your momentum carry your body into an arm support position.

In the final phase of the cast, push your body away from the bar. Keep it perfectly straight.

In performing a kip, shoot the legs forward, then, bending at the hips, thrust the feet toward the bar. Swing back, straightening the legs. Come to an arm support position.

FOR MORE INFORMATION

Getting additional information about gymnastics shouldn't be any problem, no matter what your age or where you happen to live. There are many individuals and organizations eager to cooperate. Books and magazines devoted to the sport abound.

A good starting point is the physical education teacher at your local school. She should know—or can easily find out—who is the local or regional representative of the U.S. Gymnastics Federation. This representative will be able to provide you with information on gymnastics competition in your area.

Information of this type may also be available from instructors at private gymnastics clubs. The Yellow Pages of your local telephone directory lists such clubs under the heading "Health Clubs & Gymnasiums."

The U.S. Gymnastics Federation (P.O. Box 4699, Tucson, Arizona 85717), mentioned above, is a prime source of information. Write to the organization and ask for a free materials list, which gives the names of books and booklets available and the cost of each. One of the most important is *National Compulsory Routines for Girls*, which lists and describes the skills that must be performed in official competition. It is used by schools and colleges throughout the country. A recent edition costs $4.

Similar material is available from the Division of Girls' and Women's Sports, the American Association of Health, Physical Education and Recreation (1201 16th Street, N.W., Washington, D.C. 20036). A *Gymnastic Guide* published by this organization can be particularly helpful.

The Amateur Athletic Union (AAU House, 3400 West 86th Street, Indianapolis, Indiana 46268) conducts national gymnastics competition for women in both junior and senior divisions. A copy of the AAU's *Official Gymnastics Handbook* is available from the organization for $3.

The Canadian Gymnastics Federation (33 River Road, Vanier City, Ontario, Canada K1L 8B9) is the governing body of gymnastics in Canada. Write to the organization for information regarding Canadian rules and competition.

For information on gymnastics equipment, including specifications and costs, consult catalogs published by the major equipment companies. There are two of them: Nissen Corporation (930 27th Avenue, S.W., Cedar Rapids, Iowa 52406) and AMF, American Athletic Equipment Division (200 American Avenue, Jefferson, Iowa 50129).

Several private organizations play an active role in gymnastics in the United States. The Young Men's Christian Association of the U.S., for instance. The YMCA conducts gymnastics instruction on about every one of its 1,800 local "Y's." The programs are progressive in nature, with each student advancing through various levels of achievement. The YMCA also conducts local, state, regional, and national competition in gymnastics. Contact a local branch of the YMCA for more information.

The American Turners (1550 Clinton Avenue, North, Rochester, New York 14621) is a national gymnastics organization with approximately 70 clubs or societies—turnvereins—throughout the United States. It has been in the forefront of the sport's growth and development since 1848, the year of its founding. Between 1936 and 1952, the vast majority of women who made up the U.S. Olympic gymnastic teams were members of clubs belonging to the American Turners. The organization continues to conduct instruction classes for youngsters of all ages and also sponsors regional and national gymnastics tournaments.

The American Sokol Organization (276 Prospect Street, Box 189, East Orange, New Jersey 07017) is somewhat similar to the American Turners, offering gymnastics facilities in scores of locations throughout the country. It also sponsors regional and national competition. Some local branches of both of these organizations conduct summer camps that specialize in gymnastics.

For news and general information on gymnastics, a good source is a magazine titled *International Gymnastics* (410 Broadway, P.O. Box 110, Santa Monica, California 90406). The publication features information about national and international meets, profiles leading gymnasts, and tells where to obtain equipment and supplies. It is well illustrated. A one-year subscription, 12 issues, costs $10.

The U.S. Gymnastics Federation (address above) publishes *U.S.A. Gymnastics News* six times a year. The publication contains newsworthy items concerning the sport and carries the USGF's official pronouncements and information concerning rule changes. It costs $5 a year.

Undoubtedly your local library has available one or more instruction books on gymnastics. Perhaps the most comprehensive book of all is *Gymnastics for Girls*, by Dr. Frank Ryan (The Viking Press, New York, N.Y., 1976, $12.50). A 430-page volume, the book pictures and describes over 200 different stunts, ranging from those in the novice class to advanced.

Introduction to Women's Gymnastics (Hawthorn Books, Inc., New York, N.Y., 1973, $2.95) is meant to help the beginner in her gymnastics development. Simple line drawings illustrate the text.

The Athletic Institute (Room 805, Merchandise Mart, Chicago, Illinois 60654) has published *Gymnastics for Girls* as part of its "How to Improve" series. The booklet costs $2.

GLOSSARY

BEAT BOARD—See reuther board.

CARTWHEEL—A handspring in which the body turns over sideways.

CAST—In stunts on the parallel bars, to push or thrust the body away from the point of support.

CHAINEE TURNS (CHAINES TURNS)—Turns which include a half turn in each step.

DISMOUNT—The method used in getting down from the parallel bars or balance beam.

FOUETTE—A ballet movement characterized by a quick circular kick; also, a continuous turning or revolving, made possible by the use of this kick.

FREE LEG—The leg not supporting the body's weight.

H.S. ROLL—Abbreviation for handstand forward roll.

HANDSPRING—A stunt in which the body is flipped completely forward or backward from an upright position, landing first on the hands, then on the feet.

HANDSTAND—Balancing on one's hands, the feet directly overhead.

HEADSTAND—Balancing on one's head and hands, the feet directly overhead.

HURDLE—In vaulting and some tumbling tricks, the final phase of the approach that brings the gymnast to the take-off point.

KIP—In swinging from the hands and arms on the parallel bars, a movement at the end of the swing in which the legs are thrust forward and upward. The gymnast then swings back, straightening the legs, and finishes in an arm support position.

LIMBER—A tumbling exercise which includes a momentary handstand after which the gymnast lets both legs drop forward so as to form a body arch, then pulls up to a standing position.

MOUNT—The method used for getting up onto the parallel bars or balance beam.

PIKE—A position in which the body is bent at the waist, while the legs, held straight, are pulled toward the face.

REGULAR GRIP—A method used in grasping one of the parallel bars in which the palms face away from the body as the grip is taken.

REUTHER BOARD—In vaulting and some beam tricks, the flexible board mounted on a fulcrum with one end secured which is used to gain upward motion. Also called a beat board.

REVERSE GRIP—A method used in grasping one of the parallel bars in which the palms face the body as the grip is taken.

ROUNDOFF—A tumbling trick similar to the cartwheel, but which includes a handstand and a quarter turn of the body.

SPLIT—To stretch out the legs at right angles to the upper body.

SPOTTER—The instructor who assists by supporting, lifting, or catching the gymnast as a stunt is being performed.

STAG—A body position in which the back leg, held straight, is extended to the rear; the forward knee is bent, and the arms upraised.

TUCK—A position common to all gymnastics activities in which the knees are bent and brought to the chest.

TURNVEREIN—A gymnastics club.

WALKOVER—A tumbling exercise which includes a handstand, but with the legs split in the air; the lead foot is brought in contact with the floor and then the other foot touches down in a front stride position.